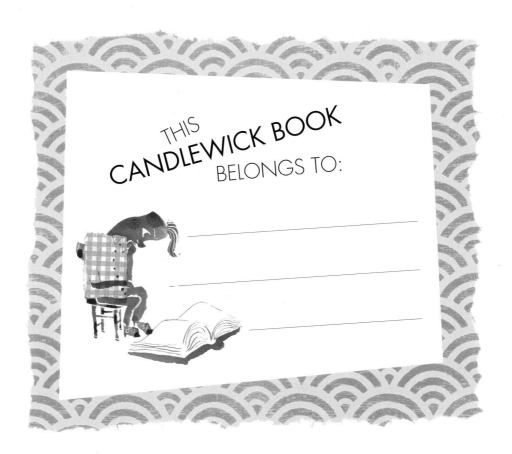

THIS
CANDLEWICK BOOK
BELONGS TO:

hey nonny hi
la la la la la
Poo poo pi d
a la la la la
a la. Whack
boom, sh-bo
a la la la

La la la la
La la la
doo.
La la la la la la
La la la la
a doo. La la
om. La la la
la la la la

a collection of
CONCrete poems

selected by PAUL B. JANECZKO

illustrated by CHRIS RASCHKA

A POKE IN THE I

```
P A U L J A N E C Z K O
P A U L J A N E C H K O O
P A U L J A A E C H H K O
P A U I J A A E C H H K O
P A U I J A A E C H H K A
P H U I J A A E C H H K A A
P H U I J R A E C H H K A A
C H U I J R A E C H H K A A A
C H U I J R A S C H H K A A
C H U I J R A S C H H K A A
C H R I J R A S C H K A A
C H R I J R A S C H K A A
C H R I S R A S C H K A A
```

CANDLEWICK PRESS

First paperback edition 2005

The Library of Congress has cataloged the hardcover edition as follows:

A Poke in the I / [selected by] Paul B. Janeczko;
illustrated by Chris Raschka. — 1st ed.
p.   cm.
ISBN 978-0-7636-0661-9 (hardcover)
1. Concrete poetry, American. 2. Children's poetry, American.
[1. American poetry — Collections.]
I. Janeczko, Paul B. II. Raschka, Christopher.
PS593.C63 C66 2001
811.008 — dc21   00-033675

ISBN 978-0-7636-2376-0 (paperback)

17 18 19 20 WKT 14 13 12 11

Printed in Shenzhen, Guangdong, China

The illustrations were done in watercolor, ink, and torn paper.

Candlewick Press · 99 Dover Street · Somerville, Massachusetts 02144

visit us at www.candlewick.com

To the memory of my father,
Frank Janeczko (1914–2000)
This one's for you, Pop.
Thanks for everything.
P. B. J.

To Richard Foster
C. R.

PAUL B. JANECZKO is a poet and teacher and has edited more than twenty award-winning poetry anthologies for young people, including *Seeing the Blue Between: Advice and Inspiration for Young Poets,* and *A Kick in the Head: An Everyday Guide to Poetic Forms.* He says, "I want young readers to see the spectacular possibilities of poetry. I'm hoping this 'poke in the I' kicks kids' imaginations into high gear and lets them run wild writing their own concrete poems." Paul B. Janeczko lives in Maine with his wife and daughter.

CHRIS RASCHKA is the illustrator of many highly praised books for children, including *I Pledge Allegiance* by Bill Martin Jr and Michael Sampson; *Yo! Yes?,* a Caldecott Honor Book; *Charlie Parker Played Be Bop; Arlene Sardine; A Child's Christmas in Wales;* and *A Kick in the Head.* He says, "Concrete poetry is the yoga of words. Like feeling your breath and your bones, you begin to notice what words and sentences actually look like. It's just like the feeling you get after a fifteen-minute headstand. And you don't even have to put on loose-fitting clothes!" Chris Raschka lives in New York City with his wife and son.

la la la la la la la la

la la la la la Sh-

la la la la la la

la la la la la la

la. Tra la la la la

h yeah yeah

TABLE
OF
CONTENTS

Notes from the Editor

Concrete poems are different from regular poems; in fact, they're a lot more playful, as you might guess from the title of this book. What are they, you ask? Well, a concrete poem can be as simple as a single word, like STOWAWAY from Robert Carola. That word becomes a poem because of the unusual way the type is placed on the page. A concrete poem can also be a selection of words arranged into a particular shape, like "Eskimo Pie" by John Hollander. The arrangement of letters or words on the page, the typefaces chosen, and the way space is used, add meaning to the poem beyond that contained in the actual words. Look at Robert Froman's "Easy Diver," for example, where the poem *is* the pigeon.

Concrete poems are often hard to read aloud (try "Crickets" from Aram Saroyan), although sometimes they are irresistible, like Helen Chasin's fourteen-line "Joy Sonnet in a Random Universe" — sh-boom, sh-boom!

Finally, these visually arresting poems are accompanied by Chris Raschka's stunning illustrations, which have a poetry all their own. So, turn the page for a dazzling, bewitching tour of thirty concrete poems from some of the world's finest visual poets and prepare for A Poke in the I.

A SEEING POEM

Robert Froman

A SEEING POEM HAPPENS WHEN WORDS TAKE A SHAPE THAT HELPS THEM TO TURN ON A LIGHT IN SOMEONE'S MIND

go

ng!

A WEAK POEM

(To be read lying down)

Roger McGough

Oh dear, this poem is very weak

It can hardly stand up straight

Which comes from eating junk food

And going to bed too late.

4

a poem moves down a page

faster than a novel

CAT CHAIR
Chris Raschka

cat

Pigeon on the roof.

Dives.

Go-

ing

fa-

st.

G O I N G   T O

HIT HARD!

O p e n s   wings.

Softly,   gently,

down.

SNAKE DATE
Jean Balderston

s m i t t e n . b i t t e n

STOWAWAY

Robert Carola

eyeleveleye

Ronald Johnson

10

I
NEED
CONTACT

L E N S E S

like I need a poke in the eye

John Hegley

SKIPPING ROPE SPELL

John Agard

Turn rope turn, Don't trip my feet, Turn rope turn, For my skipping feet.

Turn rope turn, Turn round and round, Turn in the air, Turn on the ground.

Turn rope turn, Turn to the north, Turn to the south, But please rope, please, Don't make me out.

One for your high, One for your low, Turn rope turn, Not too fast, Not too slow.

QUEUE
Sylvia Cassedy

The
life
of
this
queue
depends
only
on
you.
One
step
out
of
line
    and
    it
    all
    breaks
    in
    two.

MERGIFNIGC
TRAFF

Allen Jones

ESKIMO PIE

John Hollander

I shall
never pretend
to have forgotten
such loves as those
that turned the dying
brightness at an end of
a childs afternoon into
preludes To an evening of
lamplight To a night dark
with blanketing To mornings
of more and more There deep
in the old ruralities of play
the frosted block with papery
whisps still stuck to it kissed
me burningly as it arose out of
dry icy stillnesses And there now
again I taste first its hard then
its soft Now I am into the creamy
treasure which to have tasted is to
have begun to lose to the heat of a
famished sun But O if I break faith
with you poor dreadful popsicle may
my mouth forget warm rains a tongue
musty Pauillac cool skin all tastes
I see
sweet
drops
slide
along
a hot
stick
It is
a sad
sorry
taste
which
never
comes
to an
end

Popsicle
Popsicle
tickle
tongue fun
licksicle
sticksicle
please
don't run
dripsicle
slipsicle
melt, melt
tricky
stopsicle
plopsicle
hand all
s
t
i
c
k
y

NO PRETENDING
Robert Froman

DANDELION, BRIGHT DANDELION

You

are

not

for

any-

thing,

You

just

are.

she loves me

she loves me not

she loves

she loves me

she

she loves

she

SKY DAY DREAM
Robert Froman

WITH THEM

COULD FLY OFF

I WISHED THAT I

INTO THE SKY

FLY OFF

SOME CROWS

ONCE I SAW

```
crickets
crickess
cricksss
cricssss
crisssss
crssssss
cssssss
ssssssss
sssssts
sssssets
sssskets
sssckets
ssickets
srickets
crickets
```

THE SALMON
Douglas Florian

Could do with legs!
Just think what we
Our pearly eggs.
Upstream we spawn
We somersault!
We vault!
We jump!
Our leaps astound!
We bound!
We spring!

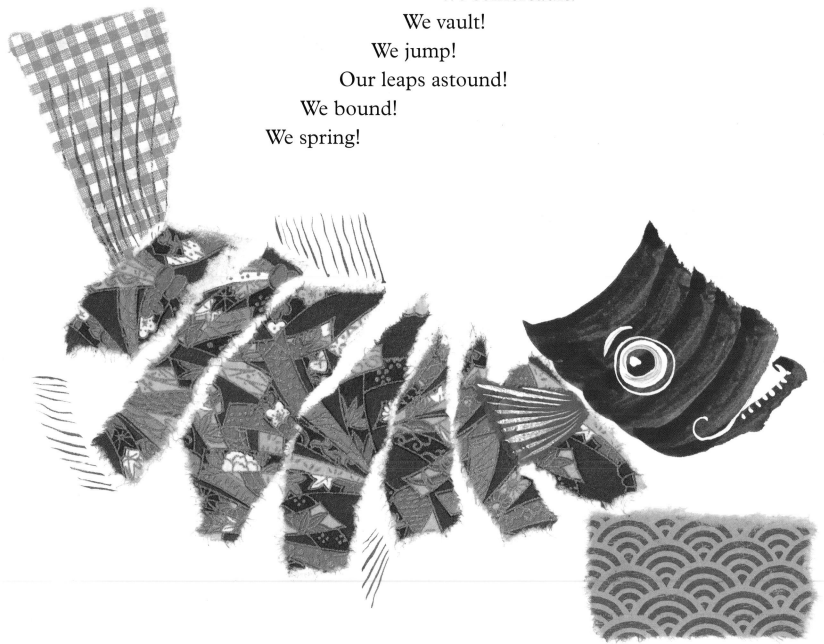

You'll see a saw

Upon my jaw,

But I can't cut

A two-by-four,

Or build a bed,

Or frame a door.

My splendid saw's

For goring fishes—

I eat them raw

And don't do dishes.

23

SWAN AND SHADOW

John Hollander

```
                        Dusk
                     Above the
                  water hang the
                        loud
                        flies
                        Here
                       O so
                       gray
                       then
                     What          A  pale signal will appear
                     When          Soon before its shadow fades
                     Where         Here in this pool of opened eye
                     In us         No Upon us As at  the very edges
                  of  where we take shape in the dark air
                  this object  bares its  image awakening
                     ripples of recognition that will
                        brush darkness up into light
      even after this bird this hour both drift by atop the perfect sad instant now
                        already passing out of sight
                     toward yet-untroubled reflection
                  this image bears its object darkening
                  into memorial shades Scattered bits of
                  light       No of water Or something across
                  water       Breaking up No Being regathered
                  soon        Yet by then a swan will have
                     gone         Yes out of mind into what
                     vast
                     pale
                     hush
                     of a
                     place
                     past
            sudden dark as
                  if a swan
                     sang
```

24

FORSYTHIA
OUT
RACE
SPRING'S
YELLOW
TELEGRAM
HOPE
INSISTS
ACTION

FORSYTHIA

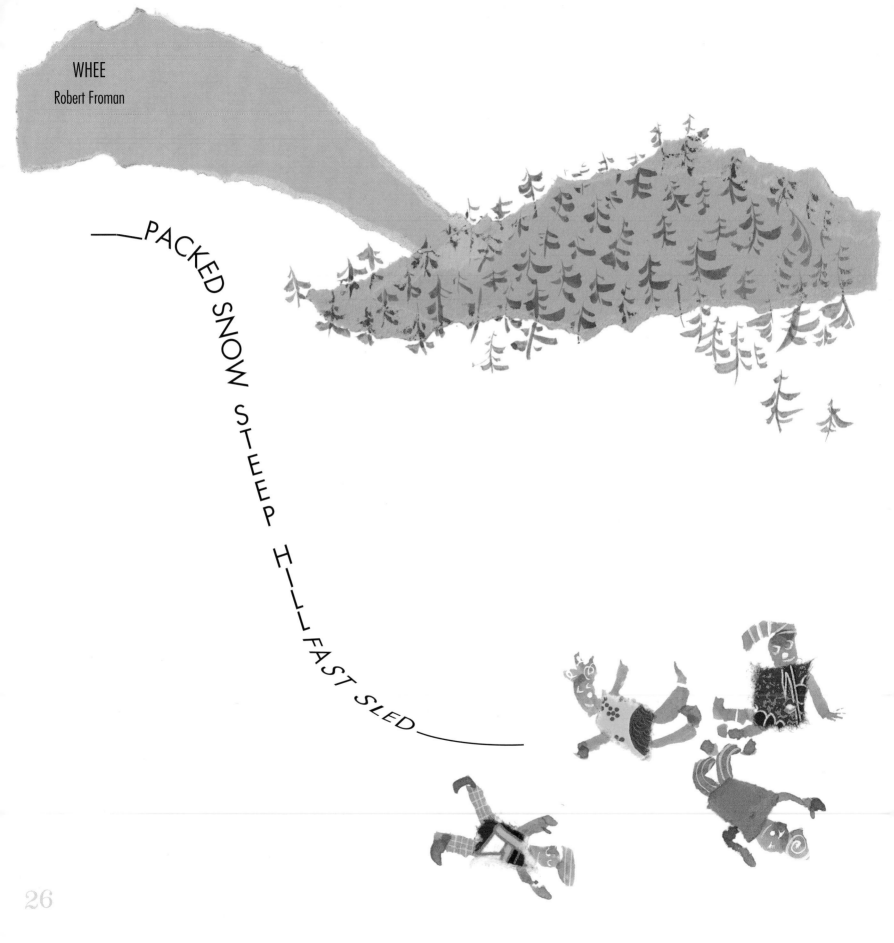

WHEE
Robert Froman

PACKED SNOW STEEP HILL FAST SLED

26

BALLOON
Colleen Thibaudeau

as
big as
ball as round
as sun . . . I tug
and pull you when
you run and when
wind blows I
say polite
ly
H
O
L
D
M
E
T
I
G
H
T
L
Y

GIRAFFE

Maureen W. Armour

A
GIRAFFE
I
S
S
O
T
A
L
L
A
N
D
HIS HEAD IS SO
FAR ABOVE HIS LEGS
HE PROBABLY CAN'T SEE

HIS   TOES   ELSE   KNEES
ADORABLE   OR ANYTHING BELOW HIS   AND ELBOWS

a   a   a   a   a
c   c   c   c
r   r   r   r   r
o   o   o   o
b   b   b   b   b
a   a   a   a
t   t   t   t   t
s   s   s   s
t   t   t   t   t
a   a   a   a
b   b   b   b   b
o   o   o   o
r   r   r   r   r
c   c   c   c
a   a   a   a   a

Ian Hamilton Finlay

29

Monica Kulling

Tennis

game I

for hours

neck won't

is a

could watch

but my

let me

31

PATTERN POEM WITH
AN ELUSIVE INTRUDER
Reinhard Döhl

Sometimes I'm happy: la la la la la la la
la la la la la la la la la la la la la la la la la
la la la la. Tum tum ti tum. La la la la la la
la la la la la la la la la la la la la la la la la.
Hey nonny nonny. La la la la la la la la la
la la la la la la la la la la la. Vo do di o do.
Poo poo pi doo. La la la la la la la la la la
la la la la la la la la la la la la la la la la la
la la. Whack a doo. La la la la la la la. Sh-
boom, sh-boom. La la la la la la la la la
la la la la la la la la la la la la la la la la la
la la. Dum di dum. La la la la la la la la la
la la la la la la la la la. Tra la la. Tra la la
la la la la la la la la la la. Yeah yeah yeah.

ACKNOWLEDGMENTS

"A Seeing Poem" by Robert Froman, from *Seeing Things* by Robert Froman, published by Thomas Y. Crowell, 1974. Copyright © 1974 by Robert Froman. Reprinted by permission of Katherine Froman.

"Visual Soundpoem" by Edwin Morgan, from *Collected Poems* by Edwin Morgan, published by Carcanet Press Limited, Manchester, England, 1996. Copyright © 1971 by Carcanet Press. Reprinted by permission of Carcanet Press Limited.

"A Weak Poem" by Roger McGough, from *Bad, Bad Cats* by Roger McGough, published by Puffin Books, 1997.

"A Poem" by Richard Meltzer, from *The Kingfisher Book of Comic Verse*, Roger McGough, Ed., published by Kingfisher Press, 1986.

"Cat Chair" by Chris Raschka. Copyright © 2001 by Chris Raschka.

"Easy Diver" by Robert Froman, from *Street Poems* by Robert Froman, published by McCall Publishing Co., 1971. Copyright © 1971 by Robert Froman. Reprinted by permission of Katherine Froman.

"Snake Date" by Jean Balderston. First published in *Light: A Quarterly of Humorous, Occasional, Ephemeral and Light Verse*, 1993. Reprinted by permission of the author.

"I Need Contact Lenses" by John Hegley, from *The Kingfisher Book of Comic Verse*, Roger McGough, Ed., published by Kingfisher Press, 1986.

"Eyelevel" by Ronald Johnson, from *Concrete Poetry: A World View*, Mary Ellen Solt, Ed., published by Indiana University Press, 1970. Reprinted by permission of Indiana University Press and the literary estate of Ronald Johnson.

"Skipping Rope Spell" by John Agard, from *No Hickory, No Dickory, No Dock* by John Agard and Grace Nichols, published by Candlewick Press, 1995. Copyright © 1991 by John Agard. Reprinted by permission of Candlewick Press.

"Queue" by Sylvia Cassedy, from *Zoomrimes: Poems about Things That Go*, published by HarperCollins, 1993. Copyright © 1993 by the Estate of Sylvia Cassedy. Reprinted by permission of Ellen Cassedy.

"Eskimo Pie" by John Hollander, from *Types of Shape* by John Hollander, published by Yale University Press, 1991. Copyright © 1991 by Yale University Press. Reprinted by permission of Yale University Press.

"Popsicle" by Joan Bransfield Graham, from *Splish Splash* by Joan Bransfield Graham, published by Houghton Mifflin Co., 1994. Text copyright © 1994 by Joan Bransfield Graham. Reprinted by permission of Houghton Mifflin Co. All rights reserved.

"No Pretending" by Robert Froman, from *Street Poems* by Robert Froman, published by McCall Publishing Co., 1971. Copyright © 1971 by Robert Froman. Reprinted by permission of Katherine Froman.

"She Loves Me" by Emmett Williams, from *Speaking Pictures: A Gallery of Pictorial Poetry from the Sixteenth Century to the Present,* Milton Klonsky, Ed., published by Harmony Books, 1975.

"Sky Day Dream" by Robert Froman, from *Seeing Things* by Robert Froman, published by Thomas Y. Crowell, 1974. Copyright © 1974 by Robert Froman. Reprinted by permission of Katherine Froman.

"Crickets" by Aram Saroyan, from *Works,* published by Lines Press. Copyright © 1966 by Aram Saroyan. Reprinted by permission of Aram Saroyan.

"The Salmon" by Douglas Florian, from *In the Swim* by Douglas Florian, published by Harcourt, Inc., 1997. Copyright © 1997 by Douglas Florian. Reprinted by permission of Harcourt, Inc.

"The Sawfish" by Douglas Florian, from *In the Swim* by Douglas Florian, published by Harcourt, Inc., 1997. Copyright © 1997 by Douglas Florian. Reprinted by permission of Harcourt, Inc.

"Swan and Shadow" by John Hollander, first published in *Poetry* magazine 1966. Copyright © 1966 by the Modern Poetry Association. Reprinted by permission of the Editor of *Poetry.*

"Forsythia" by Mary Ellen Solt, from *Concrete Poetry: A World View,* Mary Ellen Solt, Ed., published by Indiana University Press, 1970. Reprinted by permission of Indiana University Press.

"Whee" by Robert Froman, from *Seeing Things* by Robert Froman, published by Thomas Y. Crowell, 1974. Copyright © 1974 by Robert Froman. Reprinted by permission of Katherine Froman.

"Balloon" by Colleen Thibaudeau. Reprinted by permission of Colleen Thibaudeau.

"Giraffe" by Maureen W. Armour. Reprinted by permission of Maureen W. Armour.

"Acrobats" by Ian Hamilton Finlay, from *An Anthology of Concrete Poems,* Emmett Williams, Ed., published by Something Else Press, 1967. Copyright © 1967 by Ian Hamilton Finlay.

"Tennis Anyone?" by Monica Kulling. Copyright © 2001 by Monica Kulling. Reprinted by permission of Marian Reiner for the author.

"Pattern Poem with an Elusive Intruder" by Reinhard Döhl, from *An Anthology of Concrete Poems,* Emmett Williams, Ed., published by Something Else Press, 1967. Copyright © 1967 by Reinhard Döhl.

...oo. La la la la

...n. La la la la la

...a la la la la la la

...m. La la la la

...a la la. Tra la

...a la la la la. Ye...